IT'S TIME TO EAT FUDGESICLES

It's Time to Eat FUDGESICLES

Walter the Educator

Silent King Books
A WhichHead Entertainment Imprint

Copyright © 2025 by Walter the Educator

All rights reserved. No part of this book may be reproduced in any manner whatsoever without written per- mission except in the case of brief quotations embodied in critical articles and reviews.

First Printing, 2024

Disclaimer

This book is a literary work; the story is not about specific persons, locations, situations, and/or circumstances unless mentioned in a historical context. Any resemblance to real persons, locations, situations, and/or circumstances is coincidental. This book is for entertainment and informational purposes only. The author and publisher offer this information without warranties expressed or implied. No matter the grounds, neither the author nor the publisher will be accountable for any losses, injuries, or other damages caused by the reader's use of this book. The use of this book acknowledges an understanding and acceptance of this disclaimer.

It's Time to Eat FUDGESICLES is a collectible early learning book by Walter the Educator suitable for all ages belonging to Walter the Educator's Time to Eat Book Series. Collect more books at WaltertheEducator.com

USE THE EXTRA SPACE TO TAKE NOTES AND DOCUMENT YOUR MEMORIES

FUDGESICLES

The sun is shining big and bright,

It's Time to Eat
Fudgesicles

It's time for something cold and right.

A chocolate treat on a stick so cool,

Fudgesicles are the perfect fuel!

Open the freezer, take a peek,

A frosty snack is what we seek!

Wrapped up tight and dark as night,

A fudgy pop, oh, what a sight!

Peel the wrapper, hold on tight,

Take a lick, oh, what delight!

So smooth, so creamy, cold and sweet,

A frozen fudge that can't be beat!

A tiny bite, a happy grin,

Chocolate dribbles on my chin!

Lick it quick, don't let it melt,

The best cool treat I've ever felt!

It's Time to Eat
Fudgesicles

The sun is warm, the pop is cold,

A fudgy bite is pure gold!

It's chilly, creamy, soft, and fun,

Melting slowly in the sun.

Sister's got one, Grandpa too,

Mom and Dad both love them too!

We sit outside and swing our feet,

Fudgesicles make days so sweet!

Oops, sticky fingers, drips so fast!

Lick it up, make sure it lasts!

A little mess? That's quite okay,

Fudgesicles make the best kind of day!

Halfway done, I take one more,

Chocolate goodness I adore!

Each bite's better than the last,

It's Time to Eat
Fudgesicles

Why do they have to go so fast?

Just one bite left, oh no, oh dear!

My fudgy pop will disappear!

I eat it up, I smack my lips,

I even lick my fingertips!

So when the sun shines big and bright,

And you need a snack that feels just right,

Grab a fudgesicle, take a seat,

It's Time to Eat
Fudgesicles

A frozen fudge pop can't be beat!

ABOUT THE CREATOR

Walter the Educator is one of the pseudonyms for Walter Anderson. Formally educated in Chemistry, Business, and Education, he is an educator, an author, a diverse entrepreneur, and he is the son of a disabled war veteran. "Walter the Educator" shares his time between educating and creating. He holds interests and owns several creative projects that entertain, enlighten, enhance, and educate, hoping to inspire and motivate you. Follow, find new works, and stay up to date with Walter the Educator™

at WaltertheEducator.com

www.ingramcontent.com/pod-product-compliance
Lightning Source LLC
LaVergne TN
LVHW012052070526
838201LV00082B/3986